Living A Bulletproof Life

Bridget Clark

Copyright © 2017
All rights reserved.
ISBN: 0692955100
ISBN-13: 978-0692955109
All scriptures are King James Version.

DEDICATION

This book is dedicated to my husband, thank you for weathering every storm with me.

To my mother, father, grandmother, aunt, sister, brother, a very special nephew and God's servant who called me and said, "don't worry about nothing" while all my earthly belongings were actively going up in flames; thank you all for allowing me to be me in the midst of every war.

To my Texas family, thank you for the continued love and support, "Don't Mess With Texas."

CONTENTS

	Acknowledgments	i
1	Living A Bulletproof Life	Pg 1
2	Weapons	Pg 10
3	Warfare	Pg 28
4	Carnal	Pg 34
5	Mighty Through God	Pg 41
6	Pulling Down Strongholds	Pg 46
7	Casting Down Imaginations	Pg 51
8	Every High Thing	Pg 55
9	Exalteth Itself Against the Knowledge of God	Pg 58
10	Bringing Every Thought Captive	Pg 65
11	Obedience of Christ	Pg 68
12	Revenge All Disobedience	Pg 72
13	Your Obedience Fulfilled	Pg 74
14	Fight the Right Fight, Use the Right Weapons	Pg 76
15	Living A Bulletproof Life	Pg 83

ACKNOWLEDGMENTS

I am thankful for the opportunity to be used by God in every way. I look forward to the journey ahead, gleaning from the past and sowing seeds daily for an amazing future.

I humbly acknowledge that the fight has strengthened me and there has not been not one bullet that has been able to stop me from this moment of leaving this fighter's manual in the earth.

I look forward to all that God has in store for me as his vessel of honor and praise.

1 LIVING A BULLETPROOF LIFE

The title of this body of renderings came directly from a 2007 Vision. I recall waking to the visual of this book title with the subsequent graphics of a crown of thorns at the top, with blood dripping down to a cross. At the foot of the cross was a person lifting holy hands with the blood coming down as though covering the person. At the background of all of this was a silhouette of the bible.

The timing of this vision was a couple months after my God driven journey through Hell on Earth. In or around March 2006, I heard clearly that I was to go to Texas and work with this ministry. From that moment until the moment of my departure, which was about 45 days, my spirit grieved sorely. I pleaded with God that I did not want to go. At the time, I had only limited knowledge. I had no clue that I would go from undergrad to master's level in demonic studies in a period of one summer.

I can say that from my early childhood to that period of my life, I had always been a somewhat scary person. I can distinctly remember never wanting to watch horror movies with my family. When the family would gather to watch horror movies, I would either sit in the room with my eyes covered or sit in the hallway.

I now understand that I was never desensitized to the demonic realm as so many in and out of the Christian Community find themselves. The number one quoted phrase is, "it's not real." I now know without a shadow of a doubt that it is in fact a real realm.

My upbringing was in a Traditional Baptist Church. Traditional to where there were no real explanations as to why we did certain things. There were times in my adult life in this church that when I was seeking an "understanding" through asking the Pastor a question, the elderly women in the church would say that in the bible it says to "touch not my anointed."

One occurrence I recall was when I was in a meeting whereby we were conducting church business, at the time I was the Youth Director and things were changing each month, and their "touch my anointed," response was based on me asking a clarifying question to the Pastor who was moderating the meetings. This wasn't the only unproductive nuisance that left me IGNORANT, but one that stood out.

At my home church the use of the term the devil was a term thrown around like mentioning a cartoon character who was the cause of all things that go wrong in your life. There was inherently no other explanation given for his life's twists and turns other than "that's the devil," "put him under your feet." I had no real understanding or training in:

- Knowing that there was a true enemy of my soul
- No knowledge of how to fight
- No real weapons training
- No knowledge and understanding of the Fruits of the Spirit nor the Gifts of the Spirit
- No training and usage knowledge of the Armour of God

There were however, extensive messages of the Blood of Jesus Christ. Each Sunday's message would culminate with, "Jesus came to earth through 42 generations, he died on the cross, he rose on the third day with all power in his hand." Here again, I was left not knowing my role in taking on the same works of Jesus, how to apply the blood of Jesus, and how the blood gives me access to the Father. I knew that this is the way in which I received salvation.

Retracting back to my assignment to go to Texas, this was during a time when my immediate family and I had all purchased the Purpose Driven Life by Rick Warren. I remember clearly stopping at, "What Am I Here on Earth For?" I would go to God daily and say, "Lord, I know there is more to life than going to work and paying bills." I would also say, "You put me on earth for a specific purpose and this is what I need to be doing, because there is no life in just working a job and paying bills."

During this time in my life, I was seeking for God's definitive truth about the plans and purposes he had specifically for me. I did not have a full understanding of why God lead me to go work with this ministry, what I did know is that for a full month and a half prior to leaving, my spirit man grieved. The next couple of months after arriving changed my life forever. This journey was synonymous to being placed in Warfare 101 and at the end of this time of hands on training, I received my degree.

God knew what he placed in me before the foundation of the world and thereby, He knew that I would survive and like Job 13:15 I can now say on the other side of it, "Though he slay me, yet will I trust in him: but I will maintain mine own ways before him."

There was nothing that I went through able to destroy me. Not one of the enemies' tactics is able to destroy me. I am living a bulletproof life. Let's begin the training so that you too can have life and have it more abundantly.

> The thief cometh not, but for to steal, and to kill, and to destroy: I am come that they might have life, and that they might have it more abundantly.
>
> John 10:10

---

2 WEAPONS

We are in a fight! The choices are to fight or to be defeated. If we fight the right and use the right weapons, WE WIN. Most things in life are not as black and white as the life of a Christian., who chooses God's way over the ways of the world. This single choice is detrimental to our battle outcomes.

There are essential weapons that we have that help to assure us Victory. These weapons are not optional they are optimal. For 2 Corinthians 10:4 to mention the word weapons, is an indication of its need in our spiritual walk. Just as with any battle your chosen weapon has much to do with the resulting outcome.

As a young girl, I didn't fully understand the nature of bullying in its widespread context now, but all I did know was to defend myself at all costs. I've always had the mindset that if I didn't bother anyone then they shouldn't bother me. Unfortunately, as a child and even now that is just not the case. So as a school aged girl I would "retaliate."

For the weapons of our warfare are not carnal, but mighty through God to the pulling down of strongholds;) Casting down imaginations and every high thing that exalteth itself against the knowledge of God, and bringing into captivity every thought to the obedience of Christ; And having in a readiness to revenge all disobedience, when your obedience is fulfilled.

2 Corinthians 10:4-6

There was an incident where my sister and I were walking home from elementary school and she was crying about a boy who had been harassing her all day. The boy was walking up behind us taunting and teasing, as he and I began to fight I pulled off the necklace I had on and hit him.

Apparently, the necklace left a mark on him because later that evening the police came to our house and placed some sort of charges on me and told me that I had to come to the police station the next day. I remembered them saying that this occurrence would be on my record until I was aged 15. I recall thinking, he is a boy and he instigated the situation and I am the one at the police station.

As with this scenario and with our spiritual fights, we are held accountable for our responses. I did not wake up that morning and put on a necklace to use it as a weapon, but because of the situation I found myself in I used what was in my reach. This is exactly what this section of the book is about; having the appropriate weaponry in reach and ready to use at the appropriate time. I am not suggesting that using the necklace was appropriate, but with my back up against a wall fighting a boy, I used what I had available. We must be prepared for this spiritual battle we are in or we too, like I did, will use a physical weapon to fight a spiritual fight.

Depending on the era or past battles we can think of a wide range of physical weaponry. Blades, swords, arrows, spears, cannons, rifles, grenades, machine guns and many others have been weapons of choice over decades past. Even in a physical battle, a weapon that has not been properly maintained can be just as dangerous as not having a weapon.

If you were in a battle and you and your opponent have swords, it would imminently seem as though you are on equal footing. It would also appear as though sheer skill would Determine the winner of the battle.

Unfortunately, your sword is rusted and dull. You are in the heat of this battle and have the enemy right where you want him, but when you go to strike, your weapon does not break the skin, and the shock of the weapons' ineffectiveness catches you off guard. You now take your eyes off the opponent and look at the weapon to determine why it didn't work at it should've worked, or maybe even as it has worked in the past. This scenario is where many find themselves, active Christians, as well as those who have "fallen from the faith."

Many and maybe even you find yourself in the heat of day to day spiritual battles unprepared, untrained, unskilled at the art of war. The true waste of time would be to find fault, place blame, cry for days, sink into depression, or begin to lash out at everyone Around you. Not one of these actions will assist you in battle victory. Choosing to pick yourself up right where you find yourself is the only way to assure that the imminent defeat in front of you will not be the result.

Throughout the Bible, there are a large amount of scriptures that depict to us the proper ways to fight and not fight. Also, suggested in the bible are things that can be used as weapons. The things in our arsenal that we will dive into are the Armour of God, Prayer, as well as our Tongue. One of the worst things a soldier can do is to arrive at a battle without his weapons. Equally as daunting would be to arrive at the battle with the weapons and either never have been trained to use them or to have weapons that aren't properly serviced.

Armour Of God

A portion of our Holy arsenal as the Body of Christ is the Armour of God. The Armour of God consists of spiritual concepts that are divinely given and must be divinely received to accurately execute. Knowing what is available to us is only part of the battle, using what is available to us is what causes us to always triumph. Ephesians 6 lists the Armour of God. The key words that are included in this passage about the Whole Armour of God are **Truth, Righteousness, Peace, Faith,** the **Word of God** and **Praying in the Spirit**. These are spiritual weaponry for a spiritual fight.

When I think of the word truth, two scriptures instantly come to mind. The first scripture being "Jesus saith unto him, I am the way, the truth, and the life, no man cometh unto the Father; but by me." (John 14:6 KJV) The other scripture, also spoken by Jesus says, "And ye shall know the truth, and the truth shall make you free." (John 8:32) Based on the word of God, one of our weapons is Jesus; he is the truth. Matthew 1:21 says, "And she shall bring forth a son, and thou shalt call his name Jesus: for he shall save his people from their sins. The essence of Jesus coming to earth was to be able to save us from life's battles that we will encounter.

There is that weapons training I missed. I needed to know that Jesus came down through 42 generations, lived, died and rose on the third day, that I may utilize his war tactics and his name so that I may be able to fight the right fight and use the right weapons. Thank you Jesus, for being a weapon of my warfare. Thank you for the power in your name, that I have authority to utilize your name over the devices of the enemy.

Jesus is the truth. He is our high priest. Understanding the Old Testament teachings about the order of the priests helps us better understand the role, importance and need for a high priest. The old testament priests were responsible for receiving and accurately appropriating the temple sacrifices on behalf of the people. Sacrifices of animals given during these times for varying reasons were not adequate for total sin eradication.

Isaiah 53:5 states the following about Jesus, "But he was wounded for our transgressions, he was bruised for our iniquities: the chastisement of our peace was upon him; and with his stripes we are healed." Jesus offering himself as our blood sacrifice on the cross was the ultimate blood sacrifice. Through his shed blood we receive our salvation, access to God our Father, healing and heirship to the throne of God.

To simplistically explain Truth, I will use an equation: Truth = Word of God = Jesus. We often mistake facts for being the truth. It may be a fact that everything you've done up to now may have failed, but it is not the truth that you are a "failure." The truth is that according to Romans 8:37, "you are more than a conqueror." It may be a fact that no one around you has your best interest at heart, but it is not the truth that you are alone. According to Matthew 28:20 Jesus stated, "lo, I am with you always even unto the end of the world." The ability to distinguish and apply Jesus as our truth is "fighting the right fight."

Prayer

At the time of this writing in the United States, we are on high alert with the massive weaponry in the hands of North Korea. Threats of this type are rare on U.S. soil. The most notorious occurrence that threatened our country to this degree in my adult life, was 911. I remember exactly where I was during 911. I was a Proposal Writer for a technology company in Grand Prairie, Texas. I lived and worked less than 15 minutes from the DFW airport. The entire day we heard fighter jets overhead.

Fear of more attacks was the unspoken possibility. This was one of the times being away from home seemed like a dumb choice. I remember leaving work each day sitting in front of the television crying and praying for the families who had loved ones who died in this attack. Every moment felt like a pause waiting for another similar attack. I eventually had to stop watching the news in order to move on and move forward. Fear is not the correct response. Faith that God is in control will always and forever be the spiritual weapon for assured victory. What was our ultimate weapon after the 911 attack? Prayer. Believers and non-believers alike took to prayer.

Prayer is one of our spiritual weapons. Prayer is our direct line of communication with our Father in Heaven. Through prayer we employ all of the resources of both heaven and earth. Furthermore, through the Holy Spirit we access all intelligence - past, present and future. Our prayer access is through the name of Jesus. In the Old Testament, priest had ceremonial access to the earthly tabernacle. When Jesus was sacrificed, and died on the cross, Matthew 27:51 accounts that the veil of the temple was torn from top to bottom. This action gave us access to the Holy of Holies.

> And, behold, the veil of the temple was rent in twain from the top to the bottom; and the earth did quake, and the rocks rent;
>
> Matthew 27:51

3 WARFARE

Warfare is the fight. The word warfare infers that there are opposing forces. In Joshua 10, five Kings came out to war against Joshua and the Israelites. God sent hail stones from heaven and killed Joshua's enemies; so it is with us today. According to Psalm 68:1, we are to, "Let God arise and let his enemies be scattered." The dead cannot be killed. We are instructed to die to the flesh daily. The flesh can tend to rise up and exercise its' strength in times of conflict. Romans 7:18 instructs us that in the flesh, no good thing dwells.

The fight is a spiritual fight and must be fought in the spirit. Fighting flesh to flesh will always yield a defeat. Proverbs 23:7 states, "For as he thinketh in his heart, so is he." Your biggest war may be your thought life, change your thinking and your life will follow. Choose your levels and degrees of warfare by actively engaging in battle. You should in no way get ready for battle after you hear shots fired.

Be sober, be vigilant; because your adversary the devil, as a roaring lion, walketh about, seeking whom he may devour:

1 Peter 5:8

Bullet Proof Vest

Ephesians 6:11 tells us to, "put on the whole armour of God that we may be able to stand against the wiles of the enemy." What are the enemies' wiles? His wiles are his strategies. Just as the enemy stages strategies against us, we too must have strategies to minimize wounds in battle. One such strategy that is used by police and military is a "bullet proof vest." This vest is worn sometimes under or even over an officer's clothing to protect his chest from weapons of different types. This vest is made of layers of metal and other types of substances to protect officers from being killed.

The word of God lets us know that we are to be able to stand against what comes our way. Romans 13:14, tells us to, "Put on the Lord Jesus Christ." As a believer, we put on the Lord as the shelter against any opposition that comes toward us. Jesus won all victories on our behalf at Calvary's Cross. This once and for all win, encompasses anything that comes our way.

> Yea, though I walk through the valley of the shadow of death. I will fear no evil: for thou art with me; thy rod and thy staff they comfort me.
>
> Psalm 23:4

What are the bullets that are coming your way? Doubt? Hebrews 10:35 teaches us not to, "cast away our confidence for with it comes a great recompense of reward." Wanting to shout back at the taunts and character assassination of others? Isaiah 30:15 teaches us that, "quiet and confidence shall be your strength." Does it look like, "If it ain't one thing it's another?" What we see and encounter each day must be dealt with accordingly. The determination of whether or not we are fighting right is in the details of how we are dealing with the day to day occurrences. Luke 10:19 teaches us that we have been, "given power over serpents and scorpions and over all the power of the enemy and nothing shall by any means harm us." Exercise that power.

Whatever "bullets" that are launched at you there is already a blocking mechanism in the spirit that we can utilize. We must know what is available to us. We must know how and when to use these spiritual cushions against the attacks of the enemy.

Cast not away therefore
your confidence, which hath
great recompense of reward.

Hebrews 10:35

---

4 CARNAL

There are two things that are best won through the fruit of the spirit, self-control; those two things are defending and offending.

Defending ourselves in the face of conflict, confusion or any other situation places us in a vulnerable state of a battle of the flesh. Saying and doing things that offend others is another daunting situation of the flesh. Despite how we find ourselves in either of these situations, we lose. We lose because the weapons of are warfare are not carnal (of the flesh;) nor will we ever win in the flesh.

We can think of countless times and instances where we act and react based on how we feel. Our feelings are not to be factored in our responses. Colossians 3:2 tells us that we are to, "set our affections on things that are above, not on things that are on the earth." The word of God teaches us that we must die to the flesh.

Herein lies another point of inevitable victory in every situation. What is already dead cannot be injured nor killed. If we truly adopt and adapt to a way of living whereby Philippians 1:21 is a picture of who we are, we win. Philippians 1:21, is key in our arsenal which states, "For to me to live is

Christ, and to die is gain."

This discovery is the same path left to us by Jesus' death. Jesus stated in Matthew 16:25, "For whosoever will save his life shall lose it: and whosoever will lose his life for my sake shall find it." Let go of your life and gain it. When you let go, what used to be your enemies that you were trying to fight are now God's enemies. When you let go you enable Romans 12:19, "Vengeance is mine; I will repay, saith the Lord."

One of the great bible warriors, who was also known as a man after God's own heart stated in Psalm 68:1, "Let God arise and let his enemies be scattered." If you choose to die to the flesh (carnal man), God will defeat "his" enemies.

2 Corinthians 1:20 explains to us that, "For all the promises of God in him are yea, and in him Amen, unto the glory of God by us." "God is not a man that he should lie," as is stated in Numbers 23:19. We must make a conscious effort to wave the white flag on this carnal fight and truly take on the mind of Christ.

> For I know that in me (that is, in my flesh,) dwelleth no good thing: for to will is present with me; but how to perform that which is good I find not.
>
> Romans 7:18

Let this mind be in you, which was also in Christ Jesus: Who, being in the form of God, thought it not robbery to be equal with God: But made himself of no reputation, and took upon him the form of a servant, and was made in the likeness of men: And being found in fashion as a man, he humbled himself, and became obedient unto death, even the death of the cross. Wherefore God also hath highly exalted him, and given him a name which is above every name: That at the name of Jesus every knee should bow, of things in heaven, and things in earth, and things under the earth; And that every tongue should confess that Jesus Christ is Lord, to the glory of God the Father.

Philippians 2:5-11

Choosing to die daily to the flesh, is an act of faith. Either you will allow God to fight the enemies or you will continue to react in the flesh and become the enemy of God according to Romans 8:5-8. Without faith it is impossible to please God. Believe God enough to fight this spiritual battle for you in the Spirit.

For they that are after the flesh do mind the things of the flesh; but they that are after the Spirit the things of the Spirit. For to be carnally minded is death; but to be spiritually minded is life and peace. Because the carnal mind is enmity against God: for it is not subject to the law of God, neither indeed can be. So then they that are in the flesh cannot please God.

Romans 8:5-8

5 MIGHTY THROUGH GOD

Ephesians 6:10 says, "Finally, my brethren, be strong in the Lord, and in the power of his might." Our total dependence should be on the power of God. We are God's treasure in the earth. The word of the Lord states in 2 Chronicles 16:9a that, "For the eyes of the Lord run to and fro throughout the whole earth, to shew himself strong in the behalf of them whose heart is perfect toward him." God is seeking us out, to glorify his name on earth.

> But we have this treasure in
> earthen vessels, that the
> excellency of the power may be of
> God, and not of us.
>
> 2 Corinthians 4:7

In 2 Chronicles 16:7, Asa the King of Judah is being instructed that because he has relied on another King instead of the King of Kings, his enemies have escaped. King Asa was further instructed in verse 8 how large troops came against him and because he trusted in the Lord he was victorious. This takes us back to the end of verse 9 which states, "Herein thou has done foolishly: therefore, from henceforth thou shalt have wars." The story goes on that the King even after being plagued with disease sought not the Lord, but sought out physicians. We must put our trust in God, not man. We are only victorious with him. We are always defeated without him.

Then Peter and the other apostles answered and said, we ought to obey God rather than men.

Acts 5:29

Hebrews 11:6 records to us that, "Without faith it is impossible to please God, because he that cometh to God must believe that he is and that he is a rewarder to them that diligently seek him." Paul instructed Timothy in 1 Timothy 6:12 to, "fight the good fight of faith." With a slightly different wording of this passage, the message of warfare would not have been conceptualized. Had Paul stated, "be faithful," or "keep the faith," the intensity would've been lost. We must fight, a good fight, of faith in God and we can then expect God's mighty results.

The Psalmist instructs us in Psalm 24 that if we would lift up our heads, the King of glory shall come in. He further instructs us that the Lord is strong and mighty and that he is mighty in battle. We fight the right fight when we surrender and yield ourselves to the Lord to fight on our behalf.

Lift up your heads O ye gates; and be ye lift up, ye everlasting doors; and the King of glory shall come in. Who is this King of glory? The LORD strong and mighty, the LORD mighty in battle.

Psalms 24:7-8

---

6 PULLING DOWN STRONGHOLDS

The stronghold doesn't have you, you are the one doing the holding. Unforgiveness and procrastination are things that keep us in a holding position. The scriptures say, "pulling down." The imagery of pulling down strongholds can be seen through Matthew 27:51, when, "the veil of the temple was rent from top to bottom." The veil was "pulled down." In this moment, Jesus giving up the ghost, gave us access to the father. There may be many things that keep us in a "hold" due to our actions, and/or lack of actions.

Being able to forgive is a release. Holding on to past situations is a penetrable bullet that goes deeper and deeper into the flesh, while causing all types of ailments and diseases as it goes. In the same manner, accepting Jesus as our savior releases us from the guilt and consequences of sin, the same goes with walking in forgiveness in every situation.

Forgiving someone does not negate the facts, it does although lifts the burden of "holding" on to something that cannot be undone. Release yourself, by releasing that person. Reliving those situations in bouts of rage and anger is truly "fighting the wrong fight;" yet, walking in forgiveness is using a spiritual weapon.

Procrastination can be a type of hold. Living a life of, "Oh I'll do it tomorrow," is like living a life of a hoarder. There is a day of reckoning that must take place where what has been put on hold for so long festers into an even larger problem. Procrastination can be triggered by things such as fear, dread or laziness. These triggers can open opportunity for the enemy to come in and settle in our mental and resultantly in our physical environments.

Ephesians 4:27 instructs, "give no place to the devil." Actively ward off all the fears and concerns that lead to procrastination so that you can live a life that is accomplished and uninhibited. Let it all go.

I can recall when I traded the secular books I read for the bible. I literally had tons of books. All the books were about life and dealing with family members and things of that nature, but when I truly decided I wanted the ways and will of God. I packed every book that I'd purchased and placed them beside a garbage dumpster at an apartment complex. Reading those books literally consumed hours and hours of my time. The tradeoff is that for over six or more years now, I read the entire bible in a year. This replacement I made gives life and is an eternal investment. See yourself letting go as an imagery of me snatching the books off the shelf and replacing my reading time with reading the bible.

Heaven and earth shall pass away,
but my words shall not pass away.

Matthew 24:35

7 CASTING DOWN IMAGINATIONS

Imaginations are powerful and productive when they are funneled from the right source. We should constantly consider our daily sources of insight and information (images). What avenues are we engaged in the most, therein lies our source of imagination. A worthy example, is a student in a MBA program. Many groundbreaking and life changing discoveries have been birthed at this and other levels of collegiate studies.

Rightly so, due to the consistent study, research and pondering at a "Masters" level thought of business.

So goes the same fruit of many of today's teenagers. Many teenagers and those older, find themselves engrossed from morning to night with intense study, and search through mountains of research, "social media." This research is into the lives, moods and suggestions of all those who have turned themselves into "unpaid" publicists. These nations of images that encapsulate today's youth are building a story inside that young person. The fruit of these time-consuming activities are yielding results that the parents are viewing as "strange fruit."

Strange in that the link of what they as parents are instilling in their children is not the end result that is currently before them.

These two examples above are why these unhealthy imaginations must be cast down. Casting in the ideology of a fisherman is the skilled technique of propelling their hook and bait into the waters with the expectation of reeling in a fish. The same goes with our spiritual casting. The images that we are allowing to feed our thought life that are unproductive, against our teaching and training of the things of God, must all be cast away from us. James 4:7 tells us to "Submit yourselves therefore to God. Resist the devil, and he will flee from you."

It is asinine to think that we can watch live feeds of someone committing suicide and it not yield a thought of giving up. If we are choosing to watch these things, it should be coupled with prayer for the family or reading and/or quoting the word of why we shouldn't give up and "cast away your confidence" as is stated in Hebrews 10:35.

Our fight is a spiritual fight, a fight that can be won by walking in the spirit. With a goal to win, active effort should be made to guard what images are put before us, because they are shaping our actions.

8 EVERY HIGH THING

The Lord is the only one to be praised. Isaiah 42:8 states, "I am the Lord: that is my name: and my glory will I not give to another, neither my praise to graven images." There are many things that are in competition with our mind and our time. All glory, honor and praise is due to God. Exodus 34:14 states, "For thou shalt worship no other god: for the LORD, whose name is Jealous, is a jealous God." Those who's understanding has not been enlightened by the word of God may not be able to fully see present day idolatry clearly.

Cell phones are global idols. There are many who wake and lie down with their cell phones. God never intended and is not pleased with anything that consumes our time. Our carrying out his will on the earth is our ultimate task. It is the exact task that Jesus came into to the world and accomplished, "God's will." Anything that competes with our accomplishing God's will for our lives is a wile of the enemy. Scripture teaches us that we must have the whole armour of God on so that we will be able to "with" the wile, be able to stand. Similar understanding is where Isaiah 59:19 says, "When the enemy comes in like a flood." The enemy is coming, and as recorded in Luke 4:13, "he departed from him for a season."

Our charge and task at "fighting right" is to know when what is happening to us or around us is from the enemy. Ephesians 6:12 states, "For we wrestle not against flesh and blood, but against principalities, against powers, against the rulers of the darkness of this world, against spiritual wickedness in high places." Hence the "high things" that are spoken of in 2 Corinthians 10:5. Part of our victory can easily be won by resisting. We must as stated in James 4:7, "Submit yourselves therefore to God. Resist the devil, and he will flee from you." The fight is not fought in the flesh, the fight is against these "high things," that should only be fought and can be won in the spirit.

9 EXALTETH ITSELF AGAINST THE KNOWLEDGE OF GOD

Knowing God is an essential aspect of our spiritual warfare. John 8:32 says, "And ye shall know the truth, and the truth shall make you free." In John 14:6, Jesus lets us know that he is the truth.

Distinguishing between what is the truth versus what are the facts can be the key to living a life of victory versus a life of defeat. Resting our actions solely upon the facts that are presented to us and acting upon those facts, can lead us into a war that we will never be able to win. We won't be able to win because the facts are an earthbound level of knowledge, when the true war is in the spirit realm.

> Jesus saith unto him, I am the way, the truth, and the life: no man cometh unto the Father, but by me.
>
> John 14:6

The first sin of man came because God provided spiritual Truth while the enemy provided worldly facts, "You shall not surely die!" The conversation wasn't the most lethal part of this occasion, the resulting actions that were in direct opposition with God's truth is what separated man from God. We must use our spiritual checkpoint, "what did God say?" God said, "you must not eat," so therefore the fruit should not have been eaten no matter what.

Saul lost the kingdom for the same reason. Saul was in a battle situation in 1 Samuel 13 and seemingly Samuel was taking too long to arrive. Saul against the word of the Lord, offered a burnt offering. As soon as Saul finished burning the offering Samuel showed up. Samuel asked Saul a question in a similar manner to the question God asked Adam and Eve in the garden of Eden after they sinned. Samuel said, "What has thou done?" Samuel said to Saul in 1 Samuel 13:13, "Thou hast done foolishly: thou hast not kept the commandment of the Lord thy God, which he commanded thee." In verse 14, Samuel states to Saul that, "now thy kingdom shall not continue."

John 15:5 states, "I am the vine, ye are the branches: he that abideth in me, and I in him, the same bringeth forth much fruit: for without me ye can do nothing." What did God say? In the just referenced scripture God is say without me you can do nothing, we should take him at his word and do nothing without him.

We should know the word enough to know in every situation what God's word says of the situation. Ecclesiastes 1:9 shares with us that, "The thing that hath been, it is that which shall be; and that which is done is that which shall be done: and there is no new thing under the sun."

There will always be an answer in God's word. His word in our warfare is the lamp unto our feet and the light unto our path. Revelations 3:8 tells us, "I know thy works: behold, I have set before thee an open door, and no man can shut it: for thou hast a little strength, and hast kept my word, and has not denied my name." Keeping God's word is what will open the doors that no man can shut.

Thy word is a lamp unto my feet, and a light unto my path.

Psalm 119:105

Knowing and obeying God's word is what will defeat the enemies that come against us. Hebrews 5:8 tells us that, "Jesus learned obedience from the things which he suffered." We do not have to continue to suffer, because we have the knowledge that according to Isaiah 53:5 Jesus was, "wounded for our transgressions, he was bruised for our iniquities: the chastisement of our peace was upon him; and with his stripes we are healed." Accepting Jesus alleviates the adage, "Experience is a good teacher." I beg to differ; the word of God is a good teacher.

10 BRINGING EVERY THOUGHT CAPTIVE

2 Corinthians 10:5 states "and bringing into captivity every thought." For many, their life of war is the thoughts that they let run wild. Many times, we know of people who are always in deep thought. If those thoughts are not in alignment with the word, ways and will of God, then they should be immediately diverted by quoting the word of God. Our very thoughts will place us in a war that could land us in a mental institution, jail or worse.

The enemy's greatest power against us is the power of a thought. It is what we do with those thoughts that determine the path that we head down. Proverbs 23:7 teaches us that, "For as he thinketh in his heart, so is he." As we sit in thought, we must be cognizant of what is the basis of this meditation. One may say, I am not meditating. Sitting and pondering thoughts is the same process by which meditation begins.

As children of God, we are to meditate on God's word. If the thoughts are of the flesh, we need to bind those thoughts and loose the fruits of the spirit. If the thoughts are of God, we can decree that thing moves from a thought to a manifestation in the earth.

Philippians 4:8 is the sum of what our thought life should consist of, "Whatsoever things are good, lovely, of a good report, if there be any virtue, if there be any praise, think on these things." Anything outside of the will and ways of God are toxic and will only lead to death. Death of a promotion, death of marriages, death of a business deal and even premature death, as it states in Ecclesiastes 7:17.

Be not over much wicked, neither be thou foolish: why shouldest thou die before thy time?

Ecclesiastes 7:17

---

11 OBEDIENCE OF CHRIST

Obedience is adhering to all instructions that are given. In the manner that this definition is presented, one may believe that what you have not seen or heard directly may exempt you from completing the directive. Unfortunately, in our Christian walk there are no excuses for not knowing and adhering to the ways and will of God.

Hebrews 8:11 states, "and they shall not teach every man his neighbor, and every man his brother, saying, Know the Lord: for all shall know me, from the least to the greatest." Right from wrong is inherently in us to perform. Choosing whether to obey Gods truths is an option. Disobedience to God's will is sin. 1 Samuel 15:23 shares the likeness between

---

> For rebellion is as the sin of witchcraft, and stubbornness is as iniquity and idolatry. Because thou hast rejected the word of the LORD, he hath also rejected thee from being king.
>
> 1 Samuel 15:23

disobedience and the sin of witchcraft.

There are other passages of scripture that shows us that we can do whatever we want to do, but it may not be in our best interest. For example, 1 Corinthians 10:23 states, "All things are lawful for me, but all things are not expedient: all things are lawful for me, but all things edify not." We were created in the image and likeness of God to do his will on the earth. All of who we are should glorify God. Having the free will to choose and do whatever we want to is a daily battle for many who walk in the flesh.

There are many scriptures that offer to us a distinct reason why our lives should be lived in obedience to the ways and will of God.

Hebrews 5:8 says that "Though he were a Son, yet learned he obedience by the things which he suffered." Jesus came from heaven, was born and lived in the flesh. His life of no sin in the flesh is what now affords us the appropriate access to the father. The servants prior to Jesus' Calvary sacrifice did not have the liberties that we now have.

12 REVENGE ALL DISOBEDIENCE

Our position in warfare is not all passive. Passion does not allow for passiveness; neither does knowledge of disobedience. The believers quest to know the things of God and to live a life that aligns with what we know, places us in a position to revenge all disobedience. Proverbs 28:1 states that, "the righteous are bold as a lion." This boldness is not often met with acceptance.

Our charge as believers is stated in many different passages of scripture. John 14:12

states, "Verily, verily, I say unto you, He that believeth on me, the works that I do shall he do also; and greater works than these shall he do; because I go unto my Father." One instance of Jesus revenging all disobedience was in Matthew 21:12. In this passage of scripture Jesus went into the temple and drove out all of those who were selling and buying in the temple.

> And Jesus went into the temple of God, and cast out all them that sold and bought in the temple, and overthrew the tables of the moneychangers, and the seats of them that sold doves,
>
> Matthew 21:12

---

13 YOUR OBEDIENCE IS FULFILLED

We are called to hate what God hates. The way this is done in a society that calls for everyone to be "politically correct," is by adhering to Psalms 1:1, "Blessed is the man that walketh not in the counsel of the ungodly, nor standeth in the way of sinners, or sitteth in the seat of the scornful."

Many times, it would seem as though engaging in the conversation against societal wrongs is the fight we should be fighting. Contrary to that belief, it is not what we should be doing. Proverbs 26:4 discusses not engaging a fool in his folly. Being light in the midst of darkness is how we win this war. Showing the ways of God is the fulfillment of our charge from heaven.

Answer not a fool according to his folly, lest thou also be like unto him.

Proverbs 26:4

---

14 FIGHT THE RIGHT FIGHT, USE THE RIGHT WEAPONS

Isaiah 40:28-31 states, "Hast thou not known? Hast thou not heard, that the everlasting God, the LORD, the Creator of the ends of the earth, fainteth not, neither is weary? there is no searching of his understanding. He giveth power to the faint; and to them that have no might he increaseth strength. Even the youths shall faint and be weary, and the young men shall utterly fall: But they that wait upon the LORD shall renew their strength; they shall mount up with wings as eagles; they shall run, and not be weary; and they shall walk, and not faint."

Our battle position is to stand and wait. Ephesians 6:13 tells us, "Wherefore take unto you the whole armour of God, that ye may be able to withstand in the evil day, and having done all, to stand.". Ephesians 6:11 states that we may, "be able to stand against the wiles of the devil." Ephesian 6:12 explains that our wrestle (fight) is not against "flesh and blood."

Put on the whole armour of God, that ye may be able to stand against the wiles of the devil. For we wrestle not against flesh and blood, but against principalities, against powers, against the rulers of the darkness of this world, against spiritual wickedness in high places.

Ephesians 6:11-12

The wrong fight is as such: if you can name a person, place, specific date or ideology, that is the wrong fight. This one statement can eliminate a lot of headache, heartache, toil and turmoil, by understanding exactly what is being conveyed.

Our real fight is spiritual; which in order to win, we must use spiritual weaponry. Ephesians 2:6 explains to us that our salvation affords us to be "seated in heavenly places in Christ Jesus." Seated is another battle position. Does that mean that we are ceasing to fight?

Absolutely not, we are to never stop fighting. The only difference is that this is a sweat less battle. As stated in Psalm 46:10, we are to, "Be still, and know that I am God. I will be exalted among the heathen, I will be exalted in the earth!" God avenges, not us. In our seated position, we clearly see what is going on and it may anger us, but we cannot move on it. Moving on what we see takes us away from our spiritual battle position.

We must remember our weapons training. It is imperative to never lose sight of important clues discussed about our weapons. The first clue is awareness of the opponent and secondly, awareness of our imminent victory. Who am I fighting? I Win! These are the two key elements to feast on through life's journey.

Let's reflect back to our discussion about our Armour. The picture of a medieval Knight suited in shiny apparel "his armour." It appears that nothing can penetrate this fighters battle gear. This was the exact purpose and use of such gear.

The difference between us and the Knight is that the Knight uses his armour to fight a physical fight and we utilize the armour of God to fight a spiritual battle as is stated in Ephesians 6:12.

This spiritual armour consisting of Salvation, Faith, Righteousness, Truth, Peace, the Sword of the Spirit are all needed to withstand and stand against all of the enemies' tactics.

15 LIVING A BULLETPROOF LIFE

My life is bullet proof, because I rely on the word of God that teaches me: nothing shall by any means harm me, thou he slay me, yet will I trust him, and I am persuaded that nothing shall separate me form the love of God. My life is bullet proof, because I choose to die to this flesh daily. Anything that is dead, can't be killed.

In this spiritual battle, I am seated in heavenly places and I win every battle. My Life is Bullet Proof and I am living it to the glory of the Almighty God.

I've been working on this book for more than 5 years. This has truly been a work in progress. It has also been a workbook journey. As I conquered the things in this book, was I then able to write. My final deadline I set, was not met. Once the deadline was upon me, I didn't understand at the time, but there was another occurrence of impact around me that would be an integral part of this rendering. I took the biggest leap of Faith that I ever took in my life 3 years prior to the completion of this book.

For more than fifteen years, I'd been contracting myself as a Technical Writer. Over a span of 5 years, I began having exponential increases every two years. Another two years elapsed and a Business to Business opportunity was presented to me with the State of Texas. This contract was a six-figure contract, one that would secure my business in the world of Technical Writing, I would go from Bridget Clark the Technical Writer to Clark Entities, the Technical organization. There was another opportunity on the table, an opportunity that offered a severely decrease in pay, with an opportunity to affect young lives. I chose the latter. I moved back to my hometown and assisted with the opening of a 9_{th} to 12_{th} grade

Charter School.

This large leap of faith into this position, lead me into a level of warfare that I couldn't imagine even if it had been explained to me beforehand. My choice was primarily based on my life of servitude. Not only was I making less than half the salary that I've made in the past ten years, but I was working harder and more hours than I've worked in the past 15 years. I entered front line war. My leap into this position was primarily based on the impact that I could have on the lives of young people. My husband journeyed with me.

This was truly a new start for us, so much so that six months after we moved to this new "state" our house burned and we lost the contents in the house. This move from Texas to Louisiana was done so with my mother's van full, my husband's car full, my seven passenger SUV full and two u haul trucks full. Everything we'd worked for was now gone. Talk about warfare, two years prior to moving to Louisiana we had purchased a new bedroom set (custom with two chests of drawers and a dresser), new living room set, new dining room set and 2 new flat screen TVs. God was truly with us through this because we haven't missed a beat despite all this loss.

Yet, we are now faced with "starting over" with less money than we have had in years. So, we are here in this brand-new position, limited incomes, minus all our worldly possessions and grinding hard to help children. Exactly six months after the house fire, I at the helm of a non-profit organization that I founded prior to moving to Louisiana; with the help of donors and supporters put on a community back to school rally and we provided over 200 back packs filled with supplies along with digital tablet giveaway prizes to attending youth.

I channeled my loss into a gain for others. We have continued this event every year since I've moved and the event continues to grow each year. The warfare was to make me believe that I'd made the wrong choice. I can't make the wrong choice, because I've been given the assurance through Psalm 139:8 that even, "if I make my bed in hell," God is with me. Same goes with the scripture Romans 8:28 that, "all things work together for the good to them that loves God, to them who are the called according to his purpose."

My life is bullet proof because: during the entire process of writing this book, I have been in one battle after another. The common thread of them all that led to victory is that I complete the entire bible each year. The bible lends us a perfect scenario of fighting the enemy face to face and winning.

Luke 4 begins by setting the scene that surrounds the encounter between Jesus and the devil. Jesus was led into the wilderness and was taunted by the devil for forty days. During these forty days, Jesus did not eat. Jesus after each suggestion from the devil shared with him scripture.

Jesus, being the word made flesh, as explained in John 1, fought the devil face to face with the word.

Jesus was victorious in this battle, by using the word. This passage of encounter not only yields to us what specifically to use against the enemy, it yields another key for life long passage way into door after door of victory. Luke 4:13 says, "And when the devil had ended all the temptation, he departed from him for a season." This culminating passage along with the others preceding in this chapter is indicative of a few noteworthy things for us as it relates to warfare:

1. When we fight the right fight, and use the right weapons, We Win!

2. No one is exempt from fighting
3. Never stop fighting, the devil leaves only for a season.

Ecclesiastes 3:1 begins by stating, "To everything there is a season, and a time to every purpose under the heaven: Ecclesiastes 3:8 states, "A time to love, and a time to hate; a time of war, and a time of peace."

A couple of things we should ever remain cognizant of is that:

1. We are in a War
2. Knowing what season you are in (stage of war)

Getting and staying in tune with who you are spiritually is the only sure-fire way to receive the victory every time. The world says, "You win some, you lose some."

Unfortunately, for those who proclaim such, that is their truth, but for those of us who follow God's world, we proclaim and are acclaimed by something different.

2 Corinthians 2:14 says, "Now thanks be unto God, which always causeth us to triumph in Christ, and maketh manifest the savour of his knowledge by us in every place."

You will always have victory when Christ is first. Your view of your situations and circumstances will be perceived as failure or feat depending upon the lens by which it is viewed and at the time in which a situation is viewed. According to Romans 8:28, them that love God and are the called according to his purpose will have all things work together for their good. Fight right and always WIN!

ABOUT THE AUTHOR

Bridget Clark is God's servant. She has yielded her life to the work of the ministry. Bridget has been married for over 9 years. Her professional career consists of roles as Technical Writer / Proposal Writer in the Dallas Fort Worth area for more than 15 years.

Her most notable accomplishments are hailed through her philanthropic work with her non-profit foundation, Bridge It Unlimited, Inc. It this through this organization that Bridget gives back to those who don't have the resources that are needed to be successful. Her relationship with God, is what shines through the Women's events and Entrepreneurial events that she hosts/sponsors annually.

Bridget Clark is a proclaimer of God's word as an author, speaker and philanthropist.

www.ingramcontent.com/pod-product-compliance
Lightning Source LLC
LaVergne TN
LVHW051507070426
835507LV00022B/2979